Relationship Networking

The Art of
Turning Contacts
into Connections

Sandra Yancey

ISBN: 1-59852-002-4

Editor: Jan B. King, www.eWomenPublishingNetwork.com
Copyeditor: Linda Jay Geldens, www.LindaJayGeldens.com
Index: Christine Frank, www.ChristineFrank.com
Cover and Interior design: www.ToolboxCreative.com
Cover copy: Gloria Balcom, www.tnlm.com

Table of Contents

Testimonials

"An excellent handbook for networking! Whether you've done it your whole career or are just starting out, this is a "must read" for any woman who wants to take her business to new heights."

Alicia Woodhouse Hicks
General Sales Manager, ABC Radio

"Stop what you are doing and read this book before you take another step! There isn't one person in business who couldn't benefit from Sandra's networking insights and strategies."

Reneé Brown
Chief of Basketball Operations & Player Relations
Women's National Basketball Association

"I respect and admire Sandra because she has already done herself what she teaches in this important book. Now all of us have a chance to learn what makes a good woman great in business."

Hattie Bryant
Producer, PBS series "Small Business School"

"Sandra lives what she teaches. I am always amazed at how she expands her network at every opportunity. Read this book and you too will have the secret to building a successful network."

Jane E. Smith, Ed.D.
Executive Director, Center for Leadership and Civic Engagement
Spelman College

"I have seen Sandra in action and can attest to the incredible network she has created. If I had to choose only one book on networking to read, it's this one!"

Sharon Kilmartin
General Manager
InterContinental Hotels Group

"This is a must read book on how to make the "right connections" with people. Sandra delivers practical tips on how to make your "net-work" for you to enhance the daily connections we make with others."

Billy Dexter
Executive Vice President & Chief Diversity Officer
MTV Networks

"I hope women read and pay attention to this important book. Just following Sandra's ideas and concrete practical suggestions would make all of our businesses stronger."

Cindy Bates
General Manager
US Small Business, Microsoft

"I have had the privilege of knowing and working with Sandra Yancey since the beginning of eWomenNetwork, and I can think of no one better qualified to pass along advice and best practices on networking for women professionals!"

Kathy O'Neal
Vice President of Membership Services
ClubCorp

Acknowledgements

As I will say over and over in this book, no one ever makes it alone. The creation of this book is certainly a living example of the truth in this statement.

I would like to give credit to the eWomenNetwork Corporate staff for all they are and all they do. It is in knowing that I have such an incredible team beside me that I could divert my time and energy to the writing process.

A special thank you goes to my Managing Directors who lead the eWomenNetwork chapters across North America. I am humbled by our shared philosophies and their support of dedicating so much of themselves to providing a regular forum for women to come together for the purpose of helping each other succeed.

I'd like to also thank the eWomenNetwork Premier Coaches, Faculty and all the amazing women who are the members of eWomenNetwork as they have served as my Femtors™ in confirming the concepts, philosophies and approaches that led to the success in building a relationship network as well as this book.

You can imagine with a network of thousands that I could fill the entire book with names of women and men I would like to thank publicly. While pages of names are not the reason you are reading this book, there are some people who have impacted and touched my life in ways that have made me a better person and inspired me to reach higher and I want to acknowledge them.

Special thanks to some of my dear friends and colleagues who are all incredibly smart and sensational women and who have given the gift of their time and support in helping me pursue my dreams. I thank Edie Fraser, Ruth Vivrett, Sherri Hobstetter, Judy Taylor, Astrid Pregel, Lynn Connelly, Jane Smith, Dorothy Mason, Rhona Silver, Reneé Brown, Alicia Woodhouse Hicks, Donna DeBerry, Maria Coyne, Tina Chapman, Judy Bradt, Hattie Bryant, Lurita Doan, Connie Glaser, Lexi Brownell Reese, Debra Filtzer, Kelli Amick, Melanie Meyer, Cara Sjodin, Sue Malone, and Delia Passi—all of whom have supported me and my passion to help women.

Additionally, I'd like to thank some other brilliant and beautiful women who have been kind and generous in providing their time, talent and treasures. They have been so generous, and I am grateful for their support. I thank Cindy Bates, Sharon Kilmartin, Melanie Sabelhaus, Kathy O'Neal, Donna Orender, Chérie Carter-Scott, Sara Blakely, Eileen Terry, and Nely Galán.

As I like to say, behind every successful woman is a network. I am thrilled to include in it some phenomenal men. Their support is an added confirmation of my work, and for that I am so dearly thankful. Thanks to Gordon Cathey, Jerry Crabb, Darby Connell, David Brusilow, Don Netzer, Billy Dexter, John Gray, Mark Victor Hansen, George Fraser, Aaron Bernstein, Jon Gordon, Gary Lyles, John Potts and Mark Pearson.

Thanks to Jan King, for bringing out the "glow" in me and all the other aspiring and published authors.

A special thank you to Dale Martin. Her love, undaunted and relentless support of me and my vision cannot go unnoticed. I thank her for being by my side and sharing the highs and lows of starting, running and growing a business.

To my mother, I thank you for your unconditional love and for being my greatest fan. Your support of me has been as multi-faceted as a beautiful diamond, and our love and relationship is treasured and valued more than any precious gem on the planet. I can't imagine life's journey without you.

To my children, Briana and Ryland, thank you for keeping me grounded and focused on what really matters. Your authenticity is amazing and it is my greatest joy to hold your hands and experience the adventures of life together.

To Kym Yancey, my supportive husband, soul mate, and partner of 27 years and counting—in life and work—I extend my heartfelt love and gratitude to you for being the wind beneath my wings. While I could go on and on about your creative brilliance, what stands out most for me is your strength and confidence and your encouragement for me to hold true to my convictions, own my power, and share it with others. How blessed I am to experience my life and world with you!

Finally, I give thanks to my higher power, God, whose wisdom and guidance are core to my staying focused on helping and serving others and doing my part in making the world a better place.

To every one of you, I will forever be awed with gratitude.

Foreword

It is my pleasure and privilege to encourage you to read a book that will make a difference in your long-term success.

During the numerous awards dinners Sandra and I attend honoring professional women throughout the country, we are struck by the stories of how so many of these successful women start their careers going it alone. And how often it is that in their lowest moments—when they face the possibility of failure, or are going through life-shattering divorces—they call on other women for support. They reach out to their women's network and they get the help. They seek advice on business needs and gain counsel. They reach out, and in doing so, discover more energy in the women who surround them than they ever knew existed. It isn't accidental that so often these same women, with new support systems in place, go on to achieve the great successes we celebrate. Girlfriends are critical; we give one another the passion and persistence to never give up.

I have always been committed to help other women and people of color—those who would in turn help others—reach their greatest success. They need to make money to give back.

Speaking for those of us who have built our businesses and are now more capable of benevolent pursuits, I would like to share one thing: The time to network and connect with other women is now. Doing business with other women will strengthen your professional and your personal life immeasurably. We owe this connection to each other. We learn most when we learn together.

As women, we have skills and expertise to share, but much more importantly, we have insights and intuitions. Women do business differently than men do, and only when we are able to completely accept that how we do what we do is legitimate will we become all we can be. Being a woman is fun and challenging as is building a professional career. There are good times and tough times and times to celebrate and all are enhanced by sharing with a network of other women.

It is by networking that we begin to make these connections. A heart-to-heart connection with a woman who was a stranger until today could have a more profound impact on your business than you can yet imagine. Our legacies are not only of our successes, but about the quality of the relationships we build over the years. Sandra Yancey is a networking pioneer who knows how to inspire us to tap into our natural networking talents as women. As we follow her perceptive networking advice and buy from women, support women, and pass along our knowledge to the next lucky generation of women professionals and entrepreneurs, we can change the world. Accolades to my networking buddy and Femtor, Sandra Yancey, for her contributions in this book.

Edie Fraser
President, Business Women's Network
and Diversity Best Practices

Introduction

Networking is the art of creating connections and building relationships. You build a network through the reciprocal process of giving and sharing referrals, contacts, information, business, leads, ideas, resources, and advice. That's right, it's a process, meaning it has a beginning, but in this case, it has no end. And, at its most powerful, it is built on the foundation of giving first. Networking isn't something you do now and then, like only at work; networking is part of every aspect of your life. In short, networking is a lifestyle. It is not a work style. You don't turn it on or off. In fact, effective networkers don't even realize they are networking. It just becomes part of who they are. They are constantly and consistently sharing themselves. It involves a personal value aligned with the supportive behavior of being "other-focused."

Relationship networkers understand that there is something bigger, better, and smarter than any single one of us, and that is all of us. I believe the foundation of any great business is built with a collaborative effort. Success is achieved more quickly and seamlessly when we are helping each other. Remember that Lucy had Ethel, Wilma had Betty, and Thelma had Louise. We have a basic need to work together, and we know that, simply stated, working together works.

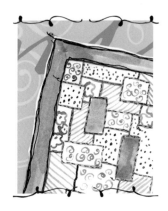

The word *together* comprises three individual powerful words—to get her. I don't believe that the feminine reference in this word is accidental. Women have known since the beginning of civilization, a million years ago on the plains of Africa, that our success would be dependent on working together and building communities. In the 21st century, these communities have morphed into our personal networks. The relationships in our network are designed to support each other and help each other succeed. As I already mentioned, they are built on a foundation of being "other-focused."

A wonderful metaphor for visualizing relationship networking is a handmade quilt. Great networkers live their lives by creating a quilt of connections. They see their role as the thread that holds the pieces of the quilt together. While they value each patch, they clearly see the beauty in the whole quilt. They share the quilt, understanding the value of lending it to others to keep them warm in their hour of need. They expect nothing in return and are comforted by knowing that the very person they have helped will add to the richness of the quilt. This same quilt also serves as a warm and cozy safety net in the networker's hour of need, for surely one of life's guarantees is that we will all have those instances in which the help and assistance of others will be required.

Networking is not about keeping score; it's not tit for tat. One of my favorite sayings is, "Give without remembering and take without forgetting." Assisting others doesn't mean you have analyzed the person you are helping and discovered that he or she knows someone you would like to know. Instead, it's adopting a belief that sometimes the best networking comes from helping someone whom you know will never be able to pay you back. To be sure, the universe seems to have a mysterious (if not deliberate) way of re-arranging itself in order to establish its own equilibrium, to give back to those who do the right thing.

Let me clarify something at the beginning: I am speaking to every professional woman—whether you own or manage a business, or are an employee of a major corporation, you are your own business, you are the CEO of your career. Think of your career as You, Inc. **You** are what you are marketing or selling. And, with the pace of change today, your future will depend less on *what* you know and more on *whom* you know. One of the greatest secrets to your future success is to understand the power of developing your network. Make no mistake about it: Everyone who "makes it" has a network.

So how does one develop a network? From networking, of course! "Network" is a verb that signifies movement and action. Networking is the process of exchanging our intellectual capital—what and whom we know—with others. The result of masterful networking, a network, is not just a list of contacts either. Rather, a network is a bevy of connections that comes from carefully cultivated relationships.

The most common networking mistake is following the misguided philosophy: "She who passes out the most business cards wins." Nothing could be further from the truth. Carefully cultivated relationships do not result from a scattershot approach, but rather require an investment of genuine interest, time and energy.

And whether you are an employee or own your business, the tips, techniques, and tools in this book will help you to build connections and attract relationships that have the potential to develop into long-term business customers and significant career opportunities.

Here's another way to look at networking. When a company buys a product, whether a copier or a fleet of cars, that company exchanges dollars in return for expected benefits from that investment. If you are employed, in exchange for your paycheck the company expects benefits from you. If you are constantly attracting new business to your organization or contributing to the retention of customers, whether you own it or not, you increase your value to that organization. This is the time to change your perspective, your paradigm, if you will, on how you see yourself and how you network. Again, you are your own business. The challenge now is to learn some new tools and strategies about how to build a relationship network.

Remember, networking is not about **me**, it is about **we**, and it takes teamwork to make the dream work. Because, truly, behind every successful woman is a network.

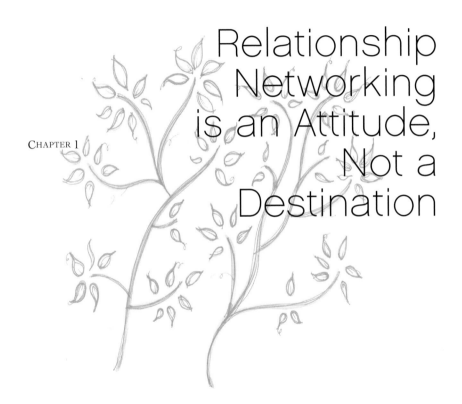

CHAPTER 1

Relationship
Networking
is an Attitude,
Not a
Destination

At one time a powerful business person was defined by his or her ability to acquire external things—fancy titles and corner offices, large staffs and fat expense accounts. But the rules have changed. Today, powerful has been replaced by influential. Influential people are defined by their ability to make things happen and get things done. How do they do this? They build solid relationship networks based on four key elements. First of all, they strategically seek out people and look for ways to establish an introduction. What may look like a coincidental meeting to the rest of the world is part of an intentional effort of navigating through the networking process, which is to converse, connect, collaborate, and create.

Each one of these elements requires relationship skills. For example, to begin to *converse* with someone, you need to be able to start a conversation by asking questions that invite information and disclosure. Then, as the person is providing this information, you look for opportunities to *connect* by identifying common ground. Common ground consists of ways in which you can relate. It could be creating a linkage to another person you both know, or a hobby you share, or a place you both vacationed, or a dilemma or challenge you both have experienced. Next, you seek opportunities to *collaborate*. An example could be by informing the person about a great book and how it helped you with a similar issue.

If you come from a place of scarcity,
that is exactly what you will attract.

Savvy networkers will follow up and follow through by sending their copy or buying the person her own. Finally, this relationship in time—some sooner, some later, and some never—will lend itself to the opportunity to *create*. This might occur when you "create" yet a new relationship by putting this person and someone else in contact with each other. In this case, your role is to initiate the conversation and create the connection. Once this is established, two savvy businesswomen will take your lead from that point on. The end result? You will have woven the web of connections known as "a thriving network."

Those with thriving networks are in a position to make things happen easily and fluidly. They remember people they meet—their names, what they do, and how to reach them. Perhaps more important, they remember the heart of conversations and the needs of those they talk to. They are constantly on the lookout for solutions to those needs, whether that turns out to be a good book, another person or an invitation to an important event. Powerful people make it their "business" to actually follow up and follow through with these connections, and so in doing differentiate themselves from the merely well-intentioned. When someone assists them, influential people send a hand-written thank-you note. They understand the subtle but oh-so-meaningful differences these touches make in today's technology-dependent society, which has come to expect that a quick email will suffice. Relationship networkers know that it is by connecting the right people with the right challenges and opportunities that companies, careers, and lives are built and made better.

There is a three-letter word that, when scrambled and re-arranged, describes the art of turning contacts into connections.

That word is *how*. Re-arranged, it becomes so much more important to know *who* rather than know *how*. The 21st century has ushered in a whole host of new realities and, the truth is, with the pace at which things are changing, you will never be able to know *how* to do everything. Those days are long gone, and they will never return. You can constantly grow your knowledge by knowing *who* to call, the very person who will know what you need to know. My point here is, despite all you've read about the power of technology and all it can do to enhance your success, it will forever pale in comparison to the power of relationships and all that they can do to enhance your success.

The art of relationship networking boils down to your ability to communicate effectively and purposefully with the right people. The best St. John suit or four-color business card won't work for you if you don't learn how to express yourself with confidence, conviction, and compassion. Couple these attributes with the ability to make others feel comfortable by mastering the arts of listening and conversation, and you have the recipe for building solid connections.

Belief in Abundance

Relationship networkers come from a perspective of abundance. Their intention is to share information, not merely gather information for their personal use or withhold information as a means of demonstrating power. To establish a growing and evolving relationship network, you must first recognize, believe, and behave according to the philosophy: "It takes teamwork to make the dream work." It is through the spirit of abundance that you demonstrate your own character and integrity by helping others whenever you can. After all, how can you expect others to do for you what you are not first willing to do for them? The point is that real relationship networkers live the law of the universe: You must give in

Your power is determined by the amount of influence you have to get things accomplished.

order to receive. You know, at a deep level, that when you give freely and without expectations, others will be there for you when you need them most. If you come from a place of scarcity, that is exactly what you will attract. I believe you become the sum average of the five people you hang around with most. I've often used this philosophy as my own guidepost when learning about others. Most people spend time with others who are a lot like them, so take inventory of those with whom you surround yourself. Are they coming from a place of abundance? Do they freely and willingly give to others, sharing information? If you are not getting the answers you desire, then you have one important decision to make: change your relationships. You can literally change your life when you change your relationships.

Asking to share something as simple as a recipe can be an eye-opening experience. I never understand women who say, "I would love to give it to you, but this recipe is a family secret." There is no place in this world for such limited thinking! How does it help you to hoard a family recipe? Does the food taste better, or nurture your family more because your friends can't make the dish exactly as you do? My mother always told me that the way to develop a real legacy is to share all that you can with others—even favorite family recipes! Now imagine how valued your friend will feel when you've chosen to share that special recipe with her: She will feel so valued, she may share her best recipe (or even her next $1-million contract opportunity) with you.

Relationship networkers know that it is by connecting the right people with the right challenges and opportunities that companies, careers, and lives are built and made better.

The old saying, "You have to give in order to receive," has never been truer than when used in the context of relationship networking. You have to believe that networking is about sharing, and expect that it will not be an even exchange at first. As you look for ways to help others, trust that others will be looking for ways to help you. One thing I know for sure, if you are too busy to help others achieve success by helping them overcome tough challenges or access transformational opportunities, then you're just too busy, period. Keep focused on the larger picture, understanding some of our greatest rewards aren't instant. Trust that the universe knows when you need its help most. It always shows up—not a minute early or a minute late.

Make time each day to pause and reflect on the number of times you have used my favorite five-word question: "How can I help you?" Consider the new connections, friends, and relationships you have established. Finish each day knowing that adopting an attitude of support and service will lead to an incurable epidemic of abundance. Think of every instance that you assisted another in accomplishing her goals and dreams as  a seed you have planted in your networking garden, then patiently watch the flowers bloom. Make no mistake about it, your network equals your power. Your power is determined by the amount of influence you have to get things accomplished.

Anytime, Anywhere is the Right Time and Place to Network

So many people think they need to find the right place to network. There is no one right place, because you take networking with you wherever you go. Networking is something that you do along the journey of life. Networking is a lifestyle you can practice anywhere and everywhere. Whether you are at an event, a restaurant, a nail or hair salon, an association meeting, or in a checkout line, or on an airplane, there is an opportunity to network, an opportunity to converse, connect, collaborate, and create. It becomes part of you. You have to say to yourself, "I'm going to hang in there and be fine, even though not every interaction is going to be fruitful and provide results." But if you hang in there, the next time might bear fruit. You are planting seeds and you never know which seeds will sprout.

Networking can be like going to church, or exercising; it requires fortitude to get going, it feels so good when you're finished, and it always produces long-term benefits and results. You just have to network, make it a way of life, and experiment with it. Give yourself a chance to make mistakes, learn from those mistakes, move on, and try again. Remember that networking is a skill and, like all skills to be mastered, it takes practice. And the more you practice, the better you get. In time, you will be able turn yourself from an amateur to a pro.

There is a lot less luck in life than we think. I'm not saying that luck doesn't play a part in success, but I do think we give it way too much credit. The universe works much more deliberately than we can possibly fathom. Luck often emerges in direct proportion to the consistent and deliberate attention we put on developing key skills and competencies. Developing relationships and growing your network takes time and intention. Trust that in the process, you will see the impact networking will have on your career and business. Again, remember that everyone who "makes it" has a slew of wonderful connections and relationships.

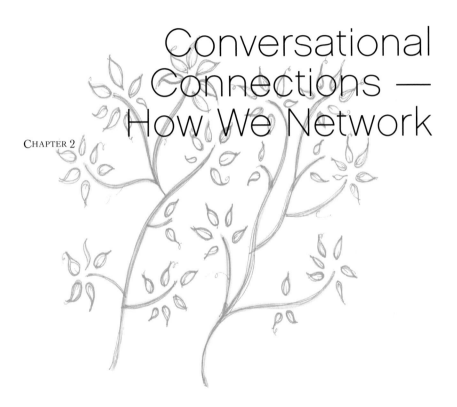

Conversational Connections — How We Network

CHAPTER 2

Networking is a communications process, and I am sure you know from your own life experiences, along with all the research that has been done, that women and men communicate differently. One is not right or wrong or better or worse; I'm simply saying that we are different. In my experience, traditional networking approaches typically follow a masculine model. Much has been written about how men build connections based on statistics and data—often referred to as *"report talk."* In the context of networking, a general conversation would typically include the man's name, title, the company that he works for, the number of employees, and the company's annual revenue. You know, a series of facts and figures.

Our #1 Competency

Women don't necessarily connect that way. Women more commonly connect by creating common ground and establishing rapport. Common ground and rapport build trust. How do we do this? Through our innate curiosity and inquisitiveness. We are curious about why and how someone got into her chosen profession, who her friends are, or where she got her earrings. These are very different types of conversations and are fundamental to building connections. Building rapport means finding common interests and developing a long-term, mutually beneficial relationship. This takes time, work, and effort. Yet, as women, we do it naturally. Given these differences, it is no wonder that so many women have struggled in traditionally male networking environments. It is like being the one Mac in a PC environment. It just doesn't easily translate.

I hope you will see that I'm not "male-bashing." That is certainly not my intention. I have many significant networking relationships with men, and I fully intend to continue to build on them. But I think one of our biggest mistakes is trying to imitate or adopt some of the male approaches. I know that I feel in complete congruence and confidence most when I embrace all of who I am as a woman, whether I'm at home or at the office. I believe that when we pretend to be like men or try to act like men, we are imposters at best.

Women command power in the new economy, and with that comes the opportunity to have our voices heard and to create lasting change.

It is time to own and take pride in being a woman—I think it's our #1 competency! It is when we have embraced all of who we are, and the fact that we can be *both* beautiful and brilliant, that we will really *glow*. Glow, by the way, is a powerful word. It is our word as women. After all, I'm sure we can all admit that while men can be many things, they just can't glow. No, *glow* is our word. And, when women glow, they stand out. Glowing is invisible, yet we can see it; we can't touch glow, yet we can feel it. Women who glow are like magnets, and their attraction is captivating and seductive. These women exude power and influence. They are typically great relationship networkers and business matchmakers because they are authentic and they seek out authenticity in others. There is no better foundation on which to make a connection, begin a relationship, or build a network.

When We Talk, They Listen

Women today are demanding environments that honor their communication styles, and companies are listening. Why? Let me share with you some surprising facts. Did you know that there are 116 million women, aged 16 and older, in the United States?[1] There are 10.7 million at least 50 percent women-owned, women-run businesses, not including the millions of home-based businesses owned and run by women. Women-owned businesses employ 27.5 million employees. That is more than all the Fortune 500 companies combined. We also generate almost $5 trillion in the $8 trillion U.S. economy. That translates into the fact that women are generating over 50 percent of all the money earned in this country.[2]

Now, not only are we earning the money, but women are determining how the money is being spent. Women make or influence 83 percent of all purchases and 91 percent of home purchases. Women buy 50 percent of all cars sold in the U.S., and influence up to 85 percent of new car purchases. Women make 66 percent of all home computer purchases.[3]

Here is an example of our purchasing power. Car manufacturers know that when your spouse or significant other is looking to buy a new vehicle, he wants your seal of approval—even if you are never going to drive the car. He wants to know that you like the particular make, style, or color. That is the power of your influence. Now, test this out, just for fun. The next time your significant other or spouse wants to buy anything, just react with "What? You've got to be kidding!" and see what happens.

It is also important to understand *how* we make purchases. It is estimated that 70 percent of all of our purchasing decisions come from the referral of another woman. What does that mean? It means we value each other, even if the other woman is a total and complete stranger. For example, I have gone to a movie with my husband and at the end of the movie, stopped off at the ladies' room. When I come out ten minutes later, he looks at me like, "Where have you been? What is going on?" I say, "Honey, I need to go to the mall. Macy's is having a great shoe sale." We bump into a complete stranger in a line and our talk turns into a conversation that will influence how we spend our money. Don't underestimate the importance of the conversational style of women and the purchasing power behind it.

I know that I feel in complete congruence and confidence most when I embrace all of who I am as a woman, whether I'm at home or at the office.

Here are a few more statistics that I think are really important to understand where women are today in our economy. Women own about 48 percent of all businesses today, and we are starting our businesses at an average rate of three to one, compared with men who are starting businesses. Forty percent of wealthy Americans (wealthy being defined as having assets of $500,000 or more) are women. Further, it is projected that women will control $1 trillion, or 60 percent of the wealth in the United States, by the year 2010. The expansion in the number of women-owned businesses with 100 or more employees, as well as those with $1 million or more in revenues, is outpacing the growth rate of all businesses of the same size.[4]

Additionally, the number of women-owned firms with 100 or more employees increased by 44 percent, which is 1.5 times faster than all businesses breaking the 100-employee mark from 1997 to 2000. The ranks of women-owned firms with 500 or more employees are expanding even faster. The number of these firms increased by 124.3 percent over the same period, nearly triple the growth rate among all firms of  this size. Further, the number of women-owned firms with revenues of $10 million or more grew by 36.8 percent, more than three times the rate of comparable-sized firms owned by men.[5]

What does this really mean? It means that the women's market is not a niche any more. In fact, I've heard it said that women are now the majority minority! Women truly command power in our economy, and with that comes the opportunity to have our voices heard and to create lasting change. Even with our incredible successes, though, we are still facing barriers. Did you know that in

2004, only 11 percent of all capital funding went to women-owned, women-run businesses? As I said earlier, women are starting their businesses at a rate of three to one over men. If we are only getting access to a small fraction of capital funding, that means we are starting businesses by using severance packages, by cashing in our 401(k) plans or by financing our businesses on credit cards.[6]

The other statistic that I find shocking is that last year, only 4 to 9 percent of all the venture capital funding that was allocated for businesses went to women-owned, women-run businesses.[7] We have limited access to capital for financing and building our businesses compared with the rate at which we are starting them. The final alarming statistic is that women who have jobs are still earning only 81 cents on the dollar, compared with their male counterparts.

Does this concern you, as it does me? With a little collaborative effort, we can speak loudly and proudly. Our collective efforts can undoubtedly change the world. Let's change the world together.

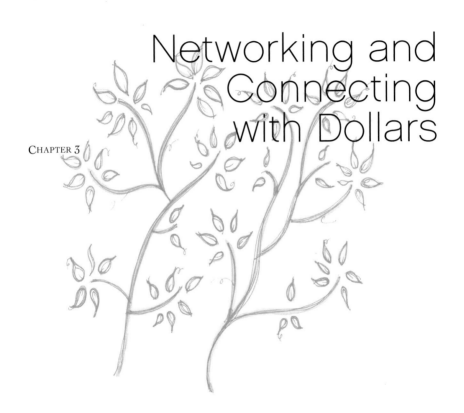

Networking and Connecting with Dollars

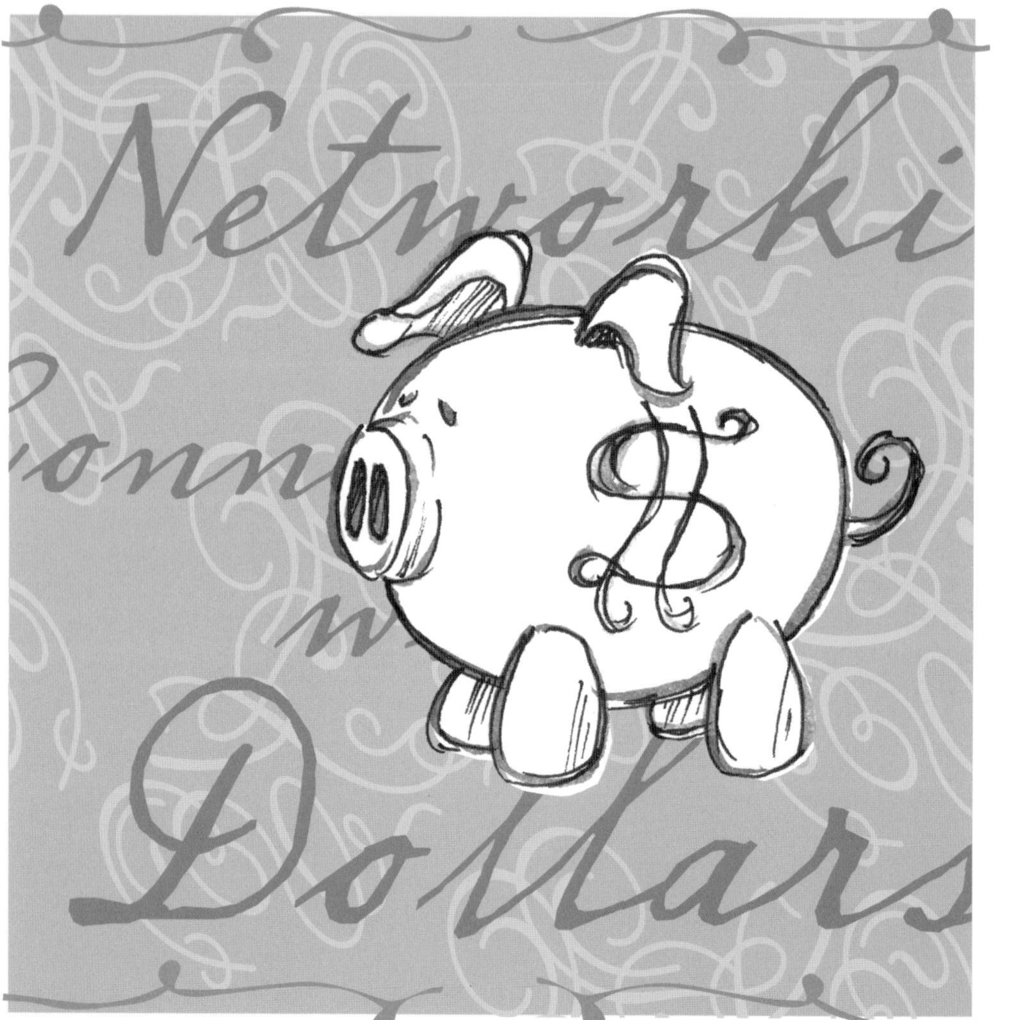

While many statistics show a great need for improvement, we are not at their mercy. We can, individually and collectively, influence these statistics in the future. Let me tell you how. As women, we must support each other. We have to be conscious about where we spend our money. We have to be much more aware of the businesses we frequent and with whom we spend our money.

Here is what I do. Recently I purchased a car. When I walked into the showroom, I was immediately approached by several male salespeople. They asked whether they could help me, and I told them thank you, but I was just looking. What they didn't know was what I was looking for. What I was looking for was a female salesperson. I am very conscious, even in a business not owned by a woman, that I want to find a woman with whom to do business so that she can reap the benefit of the commission for the sale. This is the most direct way we can help each other.

The only way we are going to be able to change the paradigm is by raising the consciousness of women and by being much more clear about how and with whom we spend our money.

How about you? Who is your doctor? Who is your attorney? Who is your accountant? From whom do you buy flowers? Whom do you bank with? Who is your financial planner? In every situation where I am spending my hard-earned money, I look for opportunities to transact business with women-owned businesses, women-run businesses, or women sales representatives who will reap the benefit of a commission from  her sales. Again, I am not male-bashing. In fact, I'm suggesting here that we emulate the way men have conducted business for years. I applaud the success they have had by supporting, promoting, and buying from each other. I am simply benchmarking their success and suggesting that this is a successful practice that clearly yields powerful results. We are long overdue in acknowledging their accomplishments and results by adopting the same model and applying it within our own gender group.

As her business grows, so does a woman's opportunities to help other women by hiring female consultants, buying from women-owned businesses, and selecting women for her boards of advisors and directors.

Corporate America today is still run primarily by men. In fact, more than 83 percent of the Fortune 500 companies do not have a woman among their five highest-earning officers. Most of those senior-level jobs are filled through networking, not advertised in the newspaper or allocated to a headhunter—at least not initially. Securing a senior-level job is about whom you know and who knows you. Men are masterful at making these important connections, a skill I think we should admire and take on as a challenge to master ourselves. Women hold only 13.6 percent of Board of Director seats at Fortune 500 companies. Of major companies that have women directors, 45.6 percent have only one woman director.[8]

Let's say you are getting ready to move and are looking for a real estate agent. You haven't bought property in a long time, so you ask your network who they would recommend. Instead of simply saying, "Whom do you know?" frame the question specifically: "Do you know a great woman real estate agent in my area?" You are giving yourself and those in your support network permission to support another woman. Try it the next time you are buying your next product or service.

One of every 11 adult women owns her own business.[9] As her business grows, so does a woman's opportunities to help other women by hiring female consultants, buying from women-owned businesses, and selecting women for her boards of advisors and directors. When you are in the catbird seat and can use your voice to influence others, know that you are exercising your moral responsibility when you help advance another woman.

Let's be clear about when a network takes on value. It is when you turn interactions into *transactions*. The purse power of women can change the world—one purse and one purchase at a time.

Who Is in Your Network?

CHAPTER 4

I continue to be fascinated by the women who seem to be able to pick up the phone and get things accomplished because of the influence they have with such a powerful network. These are women who have first names programmed to speed dial their cell phones and can just say, "Here, Sandra, I have the perfect person you need to connect with." They hand me their cell phone and the next thing I know, I'm speaking to that person. That's when you know someone's got real connections.

Never forget that in the process of helping others, we are cultivating our own bevy of connections. The strategy is to put many people in the queue of connections so that should you need something, one of them will be strategically poised to be able to help you. Any single connection may or may not have the help you need, but when you've got hundreds of people in the queue, when someone isn't available to help, you have others whom you can rely on. The likelihood, with as crazy busy as everybody is today, of a particular individual being able to be there for you, if you have only a few, is probably not very high. Nothing to worry about, though.

If you are constantly developing relationships and creating connections, you'll have a large network on which to draw.

We can divide any network into a series of constituents. By doing so, we can take an inventory of your network and make sure you have the support you need. If you find gaps, you can be on the lookout for the right people to fill those gaps. There are important constituents I want you to know about.

Huggers

The huggers are the backbone of your network. That said, don't be surprised if you find that your huggers do not fully understand what you do. They often have no real business advice to give you and typically never buy your product or service, do not work in your company, and, truth is, often have no clue about how to refer business to you. Huggers are the family and friends who love you. When you have one of those meltdown days when you are sad and don't even want to get out of bed, these are the people who are there for you. They are the ones you call at three o'clock in the morning. They hug you, support you, and just affirm you. When you say, "Life isn't fair," they say back to you, "It can be awful, can't it?" They empathize with you. You love them because you know they won't judge you, or at least won't verbalize their judgments until the perfect time to do so, not at your most frustrated moment. They make you feel affirmed and keep you rooted. All of us need these close friends and/or family members to be there for us.

Shakers

Shakers, on the other hand, are people who know you well, care immensely about you, but who also have the confidence and guts to shake you up. They will say, "Okay, you've had a bad day. But you're digging yourself in a hole now. So stop digging! Enough already! Get up, dust yourself off, square your shoulders, get out there, and get going. There is work to be done. There are people to meet. There is a whole world out there, and there is money to be made." It's not that they won't let you occasionally have a bad day. They are just more focused on helping you to get over bad times and not wallow in your misery. These shakers are instrumental to your success. They are less attached to your emotional condition and more attached to helping you problem-solve and move forward. Sometimes huggers and shakers are one and the same person, but that is rare.

Femtors

There are several other constituents who are important to your network. The earlier you build solid relationships with them, the more stable and sustaining your network will be. For instance, every woman needs at least one Femtor. Femtor is a new term you might consider incorporating into your vocabulary. I define a Femtor as a "wise and trusted woman providing knowledge, inspiration, and practical information to other women."

A Femtor is like a mentor, only coming from a female perspective and knowledge base. Just as men and women communicate differently, so it is with the mentoring and femtoring experience. I believe Femtors are an essential component to have in your network. I haven't met a woman yet who wouldn't agree that while there are similarities between men and women who own and run a business or climb the corporate ladder, there are also some very distinct and clear differences. Femtoring ensures that those differences are shared and passed on to other women who may encounter the same challenging situations.

As it is with a mentor, a Femtor is someone who picks you and whose role it is to be accessible and to provide access. These experienced women seek out ways to teach, share their wisdom, and help other women find their wings. Femtors see in you someone for whom they are willing to risk their reputations. They have decided to provide you access to information, to resources, and to people in their network. They are the catalysts who move you from one phase of your life to the next.

But if a Femtor is supposed to pick you, how do you get one to do that? Let me give you the steps: First, identify a person you admire, someone whose values are in alignment with yours, whose achievements have caught your attention, and whose style and ethics you would want to emulate.

A Femtor is like a mentor, only coming from a female perspective and knowledge base.

Now, the real work begins. Put on your "investigator hat" and find out the philanthropic passion of the person you would like to be your Femtor. That's right. Most successful people are philanthropically involved and have attached themselves to a charity or two. Search the Internet, ask their colleagues, or phone their office to find out their favorite charity. Then, find out when the next fundraiser is going to be and buy a ticket. Arrive early and get the best seat you can. When your prospective Femtor speaks, be attentive. Use strong nonverbal skills (e.g., nodding your head, clapping, smiling) to signify your interest and approval. At the end of the event, go up to the person. Introduce yourself, confirm the event's success, and tell her that you are interested in providing voluntary support at the next event. Before offering your card, write on the back, "I'd like to serve on the planning committee for your next event." Within 48 hours, follow up with a well-written letter that reiterates your interest. No response? No problem. Contact the organization directly to get involved. You can't lose. Best-case scenario is that you start the beginning of a wonderful business connection and acquire invaluable experience. Worst-case scenario, you don't make your intended connection. So what? Look at all the other connections you will make in the process. Perhaps this experience will lead you to yet another treasured connection who will see in you brilliance, talent, drive, and compassion that deserves femtoring. When one door closes, another usually opens.

None of us makes it alone, but sometimes it feels as we do. The "no one can do it like me" attitude is often called the Entrepreneurial Syndrome. Without a quick reality check, it will become a fatal disease unless the right remedy is administered. The death is usually long, ugly, and painful. While our dreams may be our own, we cannot achieve them by ourselves. It takes an entire orchestra to perform a symphony—a lone whistler can never create the richness of that sound of many instruments playing in harmony. The secret to collective success is to work less as individuals and more as a unified team—then the sum of our small collaborative efforts is significant. Just as each individual musician contributes to a symphony, we can—and will—create profound results by working together.

Role Models

Role models form another important constituency. I believe each woman should intentionally and deliberately identify two role models. Role models are different from Femtors; a Femtor is someone who picks you, and a role model is someone whom you pick. You may know them very well, or may only know them from afar. They could be living or not, but for whatever reason, you love what they represent, admire them, and aspire to be like them. My experience is that a masterful relationship networker has at least two role models—one in her personal life and one in her professional life.

For instance, my mother is my personal role model. Orphaned early, she was raised with almost nothing. When she turned 18, she came from Mexico to the U.S. in search of a better life. She met the man of her dreams and they embarked on a new life together.

My mother taught me that life is less
about embarking on a journey to "find yourself"
and more about setting goals and
charting a course to "create yourself."

After bearing three children, she received a call one night and learned that my father had been killed in a car accident—on my birthday, no less. Now a widow with three small children, one requiring heart surgery, my mother held the family together while she studied for her driving test and tended fresh vegetables in the garden. We didn't have much money in those early years after my father died, but I had everything I needed. I realize now that my mother gave me all the things money couldn't buy—love, the power to persevere, the drive to focus on what I wanted to accomplish, and the humility to give thanks and always remember to help others. I find that I rely on these attributes today as much as I rely on my ability to develop growth strategies and read financial reports. My mother taught me that life is less about embarking on a journey to "find yourself" and more about setting goals and charting a course to "create yourself." She remains a powerful role model to this day.

Eleanor Roosevelt is a professional role model of mine. While I never met her, I own a handkerchief from her estate and have framed it, along with one of her quotes, which continues to inspire me: "The future belongs to those who believe in the beauty of their dreams." I admire what Eleanor Roosevelt stood for, and her resolve to help others, even through the turbulence she endured in her marriage and the complexities and difficulties of her personal life. She left a wonderful legacy, as evidenced by the impact that she has had on my life, and the lives of millions of others.

Consummate Connectors

The final constituency in your network is made up of "Consummate Connectors." These are people who have "never met a stranger." They live to meet new people. On an airplane, they like to sit in the aisle seats, not because they want to be the first to get off when the plane lands, but because they want to increase their odds of conversation and connection. If the person sitting next to them will not respond to their conversation teasers, they want to at least have the option of speaking to the person across the aisle. Consummate Connectors are people who know people who know people. Whether standing in line at the post office or sitting in the waiting room at the accountant's office, they always seem to have found just the right person to talk to and are  completely ready, willing, and able to share that connection with you. They are usually long-time, well-established networkers, and not just in one field.

The Consummate Connector has a knack for establishing rapport very quickly. In fact, it is not uncommon for her to run to the grocery store for one or two items and come home with a dinner date for the following weekend with someone who was standing behind her in the check-out lane. Remember, you don't want to know her just because she can connect you with other great relationships you would want to incorporate in your network. The Consummate Connector is important because she can communicate your name and what you do to the thousands of people she is bound to connect with throughout her lifetime. Consummate Connectors have a knack for creating flourishing "word-of-mouth" networks. They are critical to your network, so you need to know at least three Consummate Connectors.

Cultivating New Acquaintances

Here is another vital piece of information to understand in terms of building your network: Acquaintances are more likely than family or friends to recommend opportunities and provide leads. That's right—acquaintances. Acquaintances are typically defined as being two-to-three or even four people distant from your family or friends.

Your family and friends are there to support you and they are happy for you. They will often ask you how business is going and will pat you on the back or give you a word of praise or listen to you when you are struggling, but they are not usually the ones who recommend opportunities or leads. You know…the leads… that lead to cash.

Just as each individual musician contributes to a symphony, we can—and will—create profound results by working together.

Your family and friends often travel in the same circles and therefore cannot abundantly contribute to expanding your sphere of influence—you have all the same close connections. But, like you, they each have a larger sphere of acquaintances—people they know peripherally. Your future business and expansion opportunities are going to come from the new world of these acquaintances, not from friends or family. Knowing that there is someone you need to know, and that this person is really only a few introductions away, provides another compelling reason to develop the skills, confidence and comfort needed to develop these critical relationships.

Remember, the future belongs to those who are willing to learn, unlearn, and relearn. With every experience of meeting someone new, you will be acquiring information and sharing ideas and perspectives. Through this, you will enrich your repertoire of connections and resources. So be open to new people, new ideas, new information, and new concepts. Reflect and take inventory of those things in your life that are not serving you well and paying dividends. Let them go and replace this valuable space with what will serve you better. Have the courage to take the next step.

Make sure that you have your network completely filled with the appropriate constituent base. Take note of the places where you have gaps and begin to develop your strategy for "filling in the blanks." The good news is, it's never too late to expand your network; it's never too late to establish new connections or add meaningful relationships to your life.

Have the courage to take the next step.

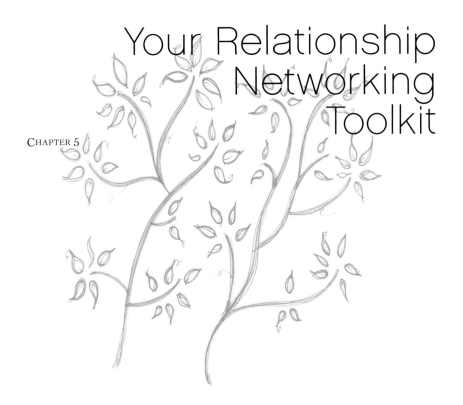

Your Relationship Networking Toolkit

Now that I have shared the context of networking, let's move into the specifics, the real skill-building tools for making great connections and building great relationships. Here is how smart women relationship networkers have mastered the skill of networking in a way that honors and supports them. Start with a networking toolkit, including some fundamentals.

Business Cards

The first item you need in your networking toolkit is a business card. Look at or visualize your business card. Which area of the card stands out? Your company name or logo, right? I hope so, because savvy relationship networkers often create their first connection by profession or industry. Why? Because it is very easy to begin conversations around what you do. At a minimum, it opens up a great leading question like, "What exactly do you do in the mortgage industry?" This question gets the other person talking. If you are focused on what they are saying, then the right follow-up questions will naturally flow.

Now look at or picture the back of your business card. I hope it is blank. You see, I firmly believe that the back side—the blank side—of a business card is the most valuable part. Why? Because it represents the space you need to write down a "gift" of how you can help each person you meet. The blank side gives you the opportunity to provide a lead, contact, resource, or other valuable information in your own handwriting as you give your card.

As you receive business cards from others, even if there is nothing you can provide for that person at that very moment, use the back of the card to jot down each person's area of expertise or some personal characteristics. Make a note of something she said she needed, so that maybe you can help her at a later date.

As you meet new people and exchange cards, here is one way to organize your cards as you collect them: In addition to making notes on the back, my secret is to bend the upper right-hand corner of the card of anyone I want to be sure I follow up with first. You can do this discreetly with your finger and thumb as you put the card in your pocket. I make it a rule to try to identify three to five people to whom I will send an immediate follow-up note. The note may simply say how much I enjoyed connecting with them; it may contain a lead, someone's name and contact information that could help them based on the conversation we shared, or the name of a book or copy of an article that would address the need they may have mentioned. Bending the corner of the card will help you sift through all the ones you collected and focus on those people you want to follow up with first.

Effective networkers are always prepared and always have their business cards available. Another favorite saying I came across years ago is: "It is better to be prepared even if there is no opportunity, than to have an opportunity and not be prepared." Keep your business cards in a convenient place so you are not digging in the bottom of your purse, or shuffling through your wallet to find them. Twenty seconds is a lot of time to waste when you could be making connections and establishing rapport.

Masterful networking is a skill, and all skills
can be learned, provided there is interest, incentive,
and incremental experience and practice.

Have you ever left a networking event with a huge collection of business cards? If you are how I used to be, the cards go from your pocket to your purse, and eventually from your purse to the top of your desk. Soon, the stack of cards starts to fall over and you put a rubber band around them. Finally, one day you simply throw the stack into a shoebox. Now you have a collection of business cards from people you don't know, can't remember where you met, and can't place a face to. It's an odd phenomenon—I know plenty of people who just can't seem to let business cards go, even if they really don't contain anything meaningful. It is the cards that I don't put a rubber band around or throw into a shoebox that have a nugget of information for me to act on, or a lead, information, contact, or resource that will make a difference in my life.

Often, people collect cards as if there were a prize for the one who collects the most. They can't wait to load the cards into their "lead generator" database or list them as "contacts" in their email system. Please note that if this is what you are doing, you have a database of "contacts," not "connections." The nuances between these two words are what database builders don't understand. Because these are cold contacts, your chances of connecting through email or direct mail are very slim. This is not how to build relationships, let alone a meaningful network. Treat each business card as the gift that it is.

Name Tags

If your experience is like mine, whenever you go to a net-working event you are always expected to put on a name tag. Now, what is the purpose of a name tag? It is simply a stick-on business card. Your name tag usually serves as the primary source for stimulating conversation at networking events. Knowing that smart networkers connect first by profession or industry, I believe that your company name should be at the top of your name tag in large letters, just like on your business card. I always print my company name in capital letters on top and then print my name as I normally would, underneath, in a smaller size. From experience I know that when all I put on my name tag is my name, or when I put my company name below my name, others don't start conversations as readily or as often as when I put my company name first. When they see my company name, it is inevitable that people invite me to tell them about my company.

Treat each business card you receive

as the gift that it is.

A great tip I can offer you is to create your own name tag and always carry it with you. That way you not only differentiate yourself from the masses, but you always present a polished and professional image. You are not reduced to wearing one of those "Hello, my name is…" stick-on name tags. They are the worst! If they don't curl up on the ends, they get stuck in my hair. If they don't get stuck in my hair, the glue on the back ruins the fabric of what I am wearing. A professional name tag emits a polished first impression.

Always place your name tag on your right lapel. That way, when you are introducing yourself to someone and shaking hands, your name tag is exactly in their line of sight.

Your Personal Introduction

Another tool to always have ready is your personal introduction—short and to the point. New connections don't need the verbal equivalent of a prize-winning novel of your history beginning with your childhood, going through your greatest accomplishments, or ending with your plans for your retirement. Instead, your job is to be able to state your name and your company, what you do in terms of benefits that you provide your customers/clients, and what you need in the next 30 days. Really, that's it. Three items. This should take you all of about 15 to 20 seconds.

The first few words you say often get in the way of easily meeting new people and establishing meaningful connections. Relationship-building cannot be done until you can overcome any awkwardness that you may feel when meeting new people. You can't stand back and blend into the scenery. You have to get engaged and get out there. And when somebody asks you who you are and what you do, you need to be able to respond. Again, your name and company, what you do, and what you need in the next 30 days.

Here is the way I introduce myself, with a smile, sparkle in my eye, and passion in my voice, confidently, and looking right at the people I'm addressing: "Hi, I'm Sandra Yancey, and my company is eWomenNetwork. I help businesswomen find each other so they can share and exchange resources, contacts, information, and business that they need to succeed. I match them with leads—leads that lead to cash. I am always looking for women who are interested in building their businesses and sharing their successes. Do you know anyone who is looking for more business?"

If you read this out loud, you will see that it takes me about 15 to 20 seconds to clearly and succinctly say who I am and what I am looking for, to invite further exploration. This initial hello is all about building a connection, establishing rapport, and giving enough information to leave open the possibility of explaining more later.

Divide and Conquer

Women, in particular, do things in pairs. Just notice the next time you are at a networking event. It is not uncommon to see a woman walk in with another woman she already knows. Then those two stand together, sit together, talk together, eat together, and leave together. And they wonder why their businesses aren't expanding! I call this the "Linus Syndrome." Just as Linus in the "Peanuts" cartoon did with his beloved blanket, they hang on to each other for comfort. When it comes to networking, making new connections and building relationships, however, this is a losing formula.

Connecting two people who didn't know each other until you introduced them is personally rewarding, and business matchmaking at its best.

Of course, it is fine to come to an event with a friend. But once you walk in that door, divide and conquer! Work opposite sides of the room for each other. Count the number of times you walk up to someone new and say hello. Count the number of times you invite someone to join your circle. Count the number of times you ask others who they are, what they do, and what their biggest challenge is. Finally, count the number of times you respond with your own compelling introduction. Masterful networking is a skill, and all skills can be learned, provided there is interest, incentive, and incremental experience and practice.

While these tools are important to setting the stage to be your most effective, they will mean nothing if you don't bring the right attitude and conversational skills to your networking opportunities. Are you ready for the next piece of the puzzle?

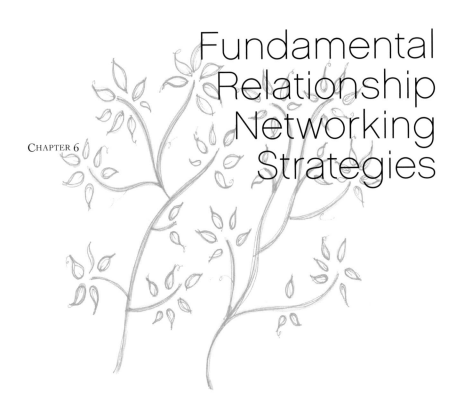

CHAPTER 6

Fundamental Relationship Networking Strategies

Relationship
Network
Fundamentals

Let me share with you my core networking strategies. When I am in my car, just as I park and before I go into a networking event, I turn the ignition off and I get myself centered. There are three attitudes that I quickly review in my mind so that I can really maximize the networking experience: setting my intention for the event, being fully present in the moment, and deciding to withhold judgments. Let me discuss each of these.

Setting Your Intention

Before you walk into any networking environment, set your intention. What is it that you want to create in this networking opportunity? Is it that you just want to meet as many people as you can and you want to pass out your business card like Halloween candy or is it that you want to have more meaningful, fruitful, beneficial conversations with people? Be a lot more interested in identifying the top three to five people with whom you can create connections than in adding dozens of email addresses to your database. You've succeeded if the conversations were meaningful enough so that you can remember their voices and the context of the conversations well enough to send them a follow-up card with an invitation for a cup of coffee or a lunch.

My mother used to tell me all the time, people will never care about you until they first know how much you care about them. How are they going to determine that? How are they going to know that you care about them? By your personal touch, of course. If you make a follow-up call asking for something or asking that she introduce you to a business contact, then she will know that you weren't genuine in wanting to create a relationship. Follow up, instead, with how much you enjoyed the conversation, how much you'd like to get to know them better, how you might be able to help them further, and how you've reflected on the conversation and the new idea that might be helpful that comes to mind. It's all about giving.

Giving the Gift of Your Presence

The gift of your presence is the most valuable gift you can give. It is essential that you do more than just *arrive* when you walk into a room—you must actually be fully present. *Showing up* means that your attention is in the room, that you are not held captive by your cell phone or distracted by your own internal dialog about what you should be doing next. The point is, wherever you are, be there completely. When someone is talking to you, concentrate on what she is saying and on how you might be able to help her. Be attentive and alert. Ask great questions and listen more than you speak. Look her in the eye. Is there anything worse than talking to someone and knowing that she is just half-listening to you because her eyes are roaming the room, searching for someone more interesting?

Don't forget that whenever you are talking to someone, you aren't just talking to that person. In fact, you are talking to her or his entire circle of influence. It could be that within that network is the perfect constituent to have in your network. Let her know by using all of your non-verbal cues, like smiling or nodding your head during the conversation.

I believe that this is an issue predominately for women. We are so talented at multi-tasking, that we can find ourselves doing it to the point where it's a detriment and not an advantage. Sometimes focusing on just one task is critical, particularly as it relates to networking and building relationships.

Reaffirm your interest in the person you are speaking with by responding with a question that follows the sequence of the conversation, not talking just to get your own agenda met. Be generous with your time and your attention.

Don't forget that whenever you are talking to someone, you aren't just talking to that person. In fact, you are talking to her or his entire circle of influence.

Let me emphasize for a moment the importance of your smile, probably one of the most powerful relationship-building tools you can have in your arsenal. A smile is universally appreciated and it is infectious. Like a magnet, your smile will attract others to you; your brilliance will keep them captivated and interested in learning more about you.

While I embrace the advancement of technology and the luxury and convenience it provides, I would be remiss if I didn't state clearly that there is no place for cell phones at a networking event. Something is inherently wrong if you don't feel that the world can survive with you away from the cell phone for a couple of hours. I can't think of a worse way to interrupt a brewing connection than the ring or vibration of a cell phone. Think how you felt at a networking event when the person you were engaged in conversation with decided that the ringing electronic device in her purse was more important than you—even before she knew who was calling. If basic manners aren't incentive enough, then imagine the impact of such behavior as potentially flushing away the connection you needed for the very breakthrough you've been seeking. Do you actually think you can get the highest return on the time and money you are investing in a networking event if you jump to respond to every cell phone melody?

I don't even carry my cell phone in my purse when I go into a networking event anymore. I don't want to be tempted by answering the phone or grabbing it when it vibrates. We haven't done our homework if we haven't put the people in place to ensure that we can do our business in a way that allows us to really give it all of our attention. If we are constantly reacting to the lives of everybody else, then how can we control and drive our own when it comes to building a network? There is no substitute for giving it our full attention. We can't half-build a relationship. We must devote the time and thought to develop our own personal infrastructure that allows the other parts of our lives to flow without us so that when we are building a relationship, we can give it our full effort.

Think about being on the reciprocal side. How many of us really want to be on the other side of the relationship when a person is only half listening, only half available to us because she is at the beck and call of everything else that is going on in her life. Think of the last time you were at lunch with a new business colleague and she said, "Oh, just a minute. This is an important call. I'll be right back with you." It's interruptive and invasive, and I think it's downright rude. And it also tells us something about that woman, that she doesn't know how to prioritize and give her full attention when it is warranted. Is she the woman we want working on our project? Is she the woman we want to introduce to our most important friends and associates?

A smile is universally appreciated and it is infectious. Like a magnet, your smile will attract others to you; your brilliance will keep them captivated and interested in learning more about you.

You can see that being fully present is critical to building relationships and to networking. But for some, this statement is easy to understand, yet difficult to implement because their habits are so ingrained. Think of the interactions you have with others as an "investment" of your time, talent, and treasures, knowing that the result will yield a thriving relationship network that will pay dividends for the rest of your life. Another way to look at it is, what dollar value do you place on your own time? Now, be honest with yourself and evaluate the types of business calls you actually receive.

If someone else could handle the calls as well as you, then you are not only wasting your own time and money by insisting on handling the interactions yourself, but worse yet, you might be throwing away thousands of potential dollars in business because of the cost caused by the interruption. If you are open to self-discovery, take the opportunity to reflect on past networking events and ponder the question, "How have my own behavior, habits and style contributed to the results I have had in building relationships and establishing connections?" Consider how the answer to this question can lead to greater awareness and better results at your next networking opportunity.

When I talk about being fully present, let me also share something with you that is generally accepted as a truth among very successful business owners: If you show up, you'll be ahead of 80 percent of your competition. If you show up on time, you'll be ahead of 85 percent of your competition. Now, if you show up on time with a plan, you'll be ahead of 90 percent of your competition. Finally, if you show up on time, with a plan and execute it, you'll make history—or should I say herstory!

Suspend Judgment

Trust that whomever you have bumped into is someone you are supposed to meet. Suspend initial negative judgments that might enter your mind. Never let yourself go to a place where you are sizing up people and prematurely drawing the conclusion that there is no one of consequence or benefit for you to meet. That is being "me-focused" versus "other-focused." If you approach each encounter with the predisposition that you are there for them, then you will always discover an opportunity to help others. With this mindset, you will become amazed at the number of times when assistance with something you need will materialize after all. It will probably astonish you how many times that the very person you are helping may not be able to help you directly. However, she may indeed be, for example, related to the sister-in-law who is in fact the ideal person you need to meet. Remember that in relationship networking, it is less about trying to *evaluate* one another and more about how to *elevate* one another. Suspending judgment becomes easier when you realize that you don't have to necessarily like everyone in your network. That is not what networking is all about. You have friends for that. Your network is going to be full of diverse people. If we believe in the true, deep-down definition of networking, it is about giving information, giving resources, giving access, giving leads, and giving clients to others. Not every woman will be your best friend. However, you can bet that everyone will have her network of phenomenal connections with women who you need to know and who need to know you. As you develop a connection and establish trust, you will increase the likelihood that she will be open to sharing, caring, and giving to you as well.

Let me share a powerful experience that I think really illustrates the point. Several years ago my daughter was on a very competitive volleyball team. Susan and Tricia, two of the girls on the team, didn't like each other, and they went out of their way to avoid each other. They would stand as far apart as possible on the sidelines and when they went to get snacks or water afterwards, they always stayed separate. This posed a problem when they got on the court. So finally in an important game, Susan had the opportunity to create a set-up play for Tricia. If she bumped up the ball, Tricia would be poised to slam that ball across the net and earn the winning point. Instead, she positioned the ball so that she didn't have to give it to Tricia, losing the point, and the game.

Trust that whomever you have bumped into is someone you are supposed to meet.

Of course, all of the girls were devastated. As the coach brought the girls together after the game to review the whole experience, she used it as a powerful learning opportunity. She told Tricia and Susan, in front of the whole team, that their personal differences were preventing the team from winning and that when you play on a team, you don't necessarily have to like the individual whose name is on the back of the jersey, but you do have to give your all for the team whose name is on the front of that same jersey.

*Remember that in relationship networking, it is less about trying to **evaluate** one another and more about how to **elevate** one another.*

As women entrepreneurs, we are on one team. We can't expect others to help us be successful if we are not helping ourselves and each other. We don't have to like each other as close friends, and we don't have to share birthday celebrations to really help each other. But we do need to help each other be successful—first and foremost, it's the right thing to do. NASA probably said it best: "This is a team and we're trying to get to the moon. If you can't pull someone up, then just don't pull them down." We're either pulling together and helping each other or we're pulling apart by withholding information. There really is very little room in between.

The Art of Conversation

the Art
of Conversation

Have you ever felt alone at an event and found yourself wandering around the room, looking for someone to talk to? Does it seem as though *everyone* but you is already standing in a group and *nobody* is willing to make room for you to enter? You can't miss that awkward silent message, "This is a private conversation and you're not invited." Don't participate in that game! I shudder to think of the lost opportunities because of such close-mindedness. When you are standing with a group and someone approaches you, take a step back, expand the circle, and invite the other person to join you in the conversation with a question. Adopt the philosophy of abundance. There really are no strangers at a networking event, only connections or friends you have yet to meet.

Talking About You and Your Business

Let's talk about networking in person and how it really works. At any networking opportunity, your goal is to begin a conversation and establish a connection. Certainly, your primary job is to be "other-focused." That said, should you pique the interest of another savvy networker, it would stand to reason that she will be "other-focused" as well. In her attempts to establish a connection with you, she will be interested in learning about you and about how she can assist you in accomplishing your goals. As a result, you want to make great use of this wonderful opportunity and be prepared to respond to her interest succinctly and clearly.

For some of us, it's tough to ask for what we want, perhaps because we aren't prepared to get what we need. It is important that we are open to new and different information. How many times have you been in a situation where someone is sharing a dilemma with you and is asking for something specific? But you've been there before and through life's experiences you know that what they really need is something very different. As you begin to share this new and different perspective you know will be very helpful, you realize that she is turning you off. She is not listening, because she has built up a wall, unwilling to hear new ideas, and she's really backed herself into a corner. Do you find you do this too?

Understand that sometimes when you are asking for what you want, there will be someone who really knows that what you need is something very different. Be coachable. Holding on to your assumptions too tightly might, in fact, cause you to miss other valuable information. Hearing different information from different people may give you a multi-pronged strategy of how to address your challenges. Maybe it isn't just one solution. Maybe it will take various elements, various different components working simultaneously and together to converge into the one piece that ultimately gets you where you are going.

There really are no strangers at a networking event, only connections or friends you have yet to meet.

Most major cities now have HOV or High Occupancy Vehicle lanes. The real purpose behind the HOV lane is to get you to your destination quickly, but your part of the deal is to take more people with you. Likewise, what really comes out of great relationships is the ability to brainstorm off of each other, banter back and forth, and be open to give and take—to take others with you on your journey. The assumption is that you know things that I don't know, and need to know, and vice versa. Therein lies the opportunity to really create a deeper connection. Sometimes you want to ask a simple question and get a simple answer. But so often our problems are way more complicated than that, and worse than that, we can't see them clearly and objectively. Simple questions and answers don't require or help you form deeper relationships. And they don't help you develop the legs or the roots you need to help you stand on your own over time.

Some of the greatest business mistakes are missed opportunities—you must be able to communicate what you want. And be available for answers that are different from what you expected.

Talking About Others and Their Businesses

One way to take care of the people you know is to be the first to promote people in your network to new people you meet. I'm not talking about name-dropping here. There is a subtle yet important nuance that differentiates whether you are trying to impress others with whom and what you know versus genuinely caring about helping to spread good news in hopes of attracting even more business on others' behalf. Be the first to tell about someone else's brand new success, whether it's a booming business or a great new client or a new, expanded location. Whatever the case, be the first to spread wonderful news. People like people who are happy for others. It is an attractive quality and one that other successful people notice. Relationship-building follows the law of attraction, so make yourself attractive to others by demonstrating your confidence and poise while reinforcing your joy in others' good fortune.

Make sure to refer people you know. Be the first to say, "I know somebody you can call for this who would be perfect for that service, or who sells that particular product." Encourage the new contact to follow up and to use your name if it will help make the connection. This is a perfect time to write the lead on the back of your business card. Not only will she have the appropriate contact information handy, but she will have all your information as well. Don't hesitate to take the card of the person whom you gave the referral to, either. You can then follow up and tell the referral to expect a call from someone new you met. Connecting two people who didn't know each other until you introduced them is business matchmaking at its best.

Smart relationship networkers don't use their Rolodex™ as a crutch to research the answer to the question, "Whom do I know?" They use their Rolodex only to extract specific information, like a telephone number or an email address. Smart relationship networkers have made it a way of life to really get to know the people behind the contact information and to connect them with others.

Listening

For many people it is difficult to walk into a room of strangers and begin a conversation, geared to hearing about the other person. Let me give you a couple of tips and techniques that you can use to start a conversation with anyone at any time. I call these the ex-words. They are example, expand, and explain. When you meet someone for the very first time and find out who she is and what her business is, ask her, "Can you give me an example of the kind of customer you serve, or could you give me an example of what kind of work you do?" Or you can say, "That's interesting, expand on that….How does that work?" Or you can say, "Explain to me exactly how you have overcome some of your biggest challenges." People will love to talk to you when you use these ex-words because you are inviting them to talk about themselves. Next, you must focus on their responses, seek to build on their comments, and look for opportunities to address a particular need they may divulge. Then, tap into your personal library of resources for a good book, consider the perfect person they need to meet, or direct them to a particular company or organization to get the answer they are looking for.

Good relationship networking is more about the follow-up and follow-through than anything else.

Now, here is another tip that will help you to generate conversation easily. Once you have asked a question, no matter what the listener says, respond with, "That's interesting….Say more." Through my Gestalt training, I learned that using the words "say more" is a wonderful and effective technique for getting people to talk more about themselves. It is a great way to acquire new information for your repertoire, your databank, and your Rolodex of the people you now include in your network.

Sometimes, more than with our words, we can successfully use vocal prompts, like "mmm" or "aah." Use your voice wisely. Remember, words represent only about 7 percent of the message; tone of voice accounts of 38 percent of the message, and body language weighs in at an astounding 55 percent. No wonder they say actions speak louder than words! Let me illustrate this important point with the following example. I could say the word "oh" several different ways and have totally different meanings. For instance, if I said, "oooh," depending on how I said it and my facial expressions, I could be signaling that I am in pain, or that I forgot something, or that I was very excited about what I just heard. It's more how we say something than what we say. Finding a balance of words and "music" (tone of voice and body language) is an important communications strategy that impacts our ability to establish connections.

Occasionally people will begin to talk to me in a language, maybe a technical language, that I don't understand. I don't need to pretend that I do understand and I certainly don't need to guess at what they are saying. I come from a place of confidence and say, "I don't understand and I want to understand. Can you say it again and in a different way?" You don't have to understand fully to say, "I really support you on this and I know some people who might know some people, so let me take your card."

Creating a network with depth and breadth means including people with all kinds of personality styles. Remember, your network won't include only those people you would invite to a birthday celebration or to your child's graduation. Likewise, your network won't include only people you would ask to help launch your

new product or invite to a fundraiser. The truth is, smart relationship builders value a diverse mix of personalities, backgrounds, and experiences because that will ensure that you have ample resources for your business matchmaking opportunities.

Staying Connected

It is fantastic to meet someone new and get excited about that new connection. But the magic is in making sure you stay connected.

Everyone walks out of a networking event with great intentions of following up and following through. The truth of the matter is, very few people will actually do it. The real work of developing a network occurs way after the networking experience ends, when you turn that connection into a transaction. A transaction in which a real and meaningful exchange of contacts, resources, and information occurs long after your initial meeting.

I have discovered that one of the reasons we don't stay connected as we should is that we feel that what we have to say or what we want to do for someone else really isn't that significant. One of my favorite sayings is this: "If you think that you're too small to make a difference, then you haven't been in bed with a mosquito." The point here is, never doubt, not even for a second, that the little things that you do can sprout something of significance for someone else. Small things turn into big things. Just like small talk sometimes turns into big talk.

If you think to yourself on occasion, "I've got so many problems of my own, how can I possibly help someone else?" let me tell you something: My mother used to say to me, "Sandra, the best way to get rid of your own problems is to help people solve their problems."

Good relationship networking is more about the follow-up and follow-through than anything else. Your future and fortune are directly linked to your follow-up. There is no magic to following up—you just do it by making a commitment. Set an intention to consistently connect with three people after the event. Do it in a way that you use my five favorite words: How can I help you? Do it with fun and excitement and vigor and know that when you're helping other people, you are positioning yourself for other people to help you.

Once you have the contact, once you have the business card, once you have received a lead, it is about following up with the person with whom you are hoping to do business. And it is about following up with the person who may have just referred you. It is also about following up with your Femtor, mentor or role model— even if you may not have contacted him or her in ten or fifteen years. What a wonderful experience for that person to receive a phone call or a card from you sharing that your experiences with them long ago led to the success that you are experiencing today.

The most important kind of follow-up is follow-through. Do what you say you will do. And when in doubt, under-promise and over-deliver. I'll bet you can remember more than one situation in which someone "promised" you something and never came through. Maybe it was something really important to you, and maybe it should have been easy for that person to keep his or her promise. There is a natural temptation to make a promise on the spur of the moment. But a promise not kept can undermine the trust in a relationship and disconnect an important connection, so if you say you will make an introduction or send an email on Monday, do it.

The best way to get rid of your own problems is to help people solve their problems.

Expressing Appreciation

Thank-you notes are not an option; they are an essential. I am not talking emails here. There is nothing more personal than a handwritten thank-you note. I put stamps on the envelopes and take them wherever I go. Why? Because I spend so much of my life waiting—in lines, in offices, on an airplane, and in my car. What better use of time than writing a simple note: "Hey, I am just thinking about you. We haven't talked in a while, but just want you to know you have been in my thoughts." Or, "Here is a business card. I ran into this person, I told them about you, and I think you ought to follow up. It could be a great opportunity and business lead for you." It is about staying connected and letting someone know you are thinking about her. How many people do you hear from only when they need something? That is not net-working. That is what I call net-begging. You don't want to be the person others avoid by checking Caller ID, seeing your name, and letting your calls forward to voice mail. You want to be the person whose phone calls others are eager to answer.

Make sure you take special care of the people who've gone out of their way to bring you business. Again, sending thank-you cards, a gift basket, taking them out to lunch, and following up by referring business to them are all important gestures. I like to buy $5 gift cards at the corner coffee house and include them with my thank-you notes. I express my appreciation and encourage them to have their favorite "Cuppa Joe" on me.

Do what you say you will do. And when in doubt, under-promise and over-deliver.

Think of these relationships as bank accounts. When you tap someone else for a contact or a resource or help, what you have done is made a withdrawal. You want to add value to these rela-tionships. So not only do you give back to equal the amount you have withdrawn, but you make an additional deposit. Look out for opportunities to refer business to them, to say something good about them, to constantly make deposits to that relationship. That is how you take care of the people you know…and the people you owe.

The opportunity is there to network generously by sharing yourself, your information, your contacts, and your resources. Then you'll be in a great position to reap all the wonderful rewards associated with doing that for years to come.

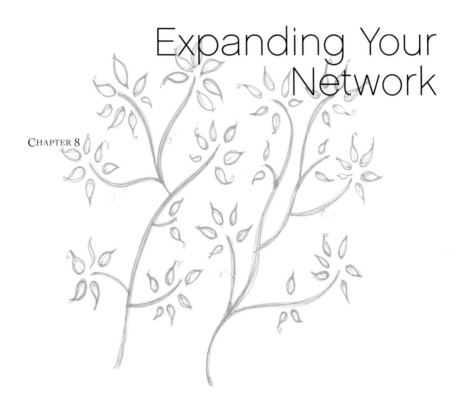

Expanding Your Network

CHAPTER 8

Expanding your Network

Many women express the frustration: "How can I be out networking when I've got a business to run?" If you are a woman like me, you are juggling a lot. You are wearing many hats, sometimes all at once. The truth is, we can't be everywhere all the time. A common entrepreneurial problem is that we are so busy working "in" the business, that we aren't working "on" the business. Also, we don't always tap the resources we need and put the tools in place so that our business can grow in our absence.

Making the Commitment to Network

There is no substitute for consistent and constant networking, meeting new people, building new connections, and gaining new ideas. You have to have your face in the place. You've got to be seen on the scene. You must circulate to percolate. You can't worry that every interaction is going to reap a particular reward for you. You go with the perspective of, I am going to give and I know that I will receive tenfold over time, maybe in a way I never expected.

Relationship networking is about aligning with others and being available to help.

If meeting strangers is about as exciting for you as going to the dentist, then I have one piece of direct advice: Think in advance, way in advance, about creating these opportunities, month in and month out. What regular monthly meetings are you committed to attending? What annual events will you schedule over the next year, even though it means time away from the office? Making time to invest in your intellectual capital and building your business acumen is a fundamental requirement in order to continue to expand, grow, and scale your company. This is a vital part of your job, but in the battle of the day-to-day, it's easy to lose sight of just how important this is.

Being an entrepreneur is about living on the edge. To the degree possible, you must calculate your risks. But, when you are breaking new ground or working your way into uncharted waters, you won't have absolute guarantees. There will always be unknowns. My advice is to get comfortable with the discomfort of the unknown. Put some tools, techniques, and practices in place to help you. I have found that nothing provides better support or builds a stronger safety net than a powerful network. So, practice initiating conversations with strangers. Remember to use your ex-words, such as, "Can you give me an example? Can you explain that to me? Can you expand on that?" Don't forget to use, "Say more." Believe me, when you practice it over and over, it gets easier and easier. Be the bearer of good news, and come from a place of abundance.

Creating the support and cauldron of new ideas is a challenge to all business women, but the best ones give it the priority it deserves.

Putting Your Intentions to the Test

Being a committed participant at regular events and staying connected with old friends and business associates are not just about getting your needs met. Relationship networking is about aligning with others and being available to help. You have to trust that when you give something away to someone, you've actually gained a deposit to your networking bank account, which will pay dividends for years to come.

You get what you give, and although it is not always an exact exchange and it doesn't always happen at a time of your choosing, it is a law of the universe you can count on.

I'll never forget this example from when I had my own consulting firm. I had wanted to get in to do business with a particular Fortune 100 company for a long, long time. I had done a lot of sales training for them, but I wanted to get into their corporate office and do some major re-engineering work. Finally, one day, the phone rang and sure enough, it was their corporate office. But the project that was outlined for me was way over my head, out of my skill-set and beyond my competencies. Yet when I refused the work, I was caught off-guard when the client asked, "Do you know someone else who could do this work?" The truth of the matter is, I did know someone, but I got caught in a moment of scarcity. I was coming from a place of fear, and so I did not give her that person's name. When I hung up, I thought about it and realized that I was afraid. I was afraid that if I gave her name, she might develop a wonderful relationship with the client and then I would forever be out of the loop. What I failed to realize was that the client was going to find someone else anyway, whether it was someone I knew or not.

After a few days I called the client back and said, "You know, I have been thinking about this, and I do have a name for you." I referred a friend and colleague who I knew would do a great job. In the end, that person got a significant assignment and made a tremendous amount of money. Almost five years later, that friend of mine decided to leave his own consulting business and go back into corporate America, and he joined a large company. The irony is that one day my phone rang, and it was him. And he said to me, "Sandra, I've got

the perfect assignment for you." And five years later, that important referral he gave me had the value of almost the same amount of money as the referral that I had given to him five years before. You get what you give, and although it is not always an exact exchange and it doesn't always happen at a time of your choosing, it is a law of the universe you can count on.

Attracting Business While Doing Business

As important as it is to be committed to personal networking, you can't be in enough places at once personally to extend your reach to everyone who needs to know you.

It is true that one of your core responsibilities is to constantly and consistently build new relationships and establish great connections. You also have a responsibility to make it easy for other people to find you and do business with you. You must have a strong business presence other than yourself.

I found myself in this very same predicament, which is the reason I started eWomenNetwork. I wanted a place where I could converse, connect, collaborate, and create with dynamic, brilliant, business-minded women for the purposes of sharing information and supporting each other. That is the "high touch" side of the eWomenNetwork business. But I also knew that I needed a strong web presence. I needed a way for people who remembered me, but maybe had lost my business card, to find out about me. That became the "high tech" side of eWomenNetwork.

Did you know that up to 80 percent of business opportunities are lost because people either can't find you or don't know you exist? This is true whether they want to buy from you directly or want to refer you to someone else. The problem that most entrepreneurs face is that they usually don't have the marketing muscle or budget to brand their businesses or web sites. One of the primary purposes of the eWomenNetwork web site is to brand it on behalf of our members as a place to find competent and caring business women who can address any customer's need.

There are many ways to make connections worldwide besides a web presence. These include publishing books and other informational products, writing articles and public speaking, and offering teleclasses, seminars and keynotes.

How many more people will be in place to direct clients to you if they become fully familiar with your story and your work because they've read your book, attended your seminar, or heard you give a keynote? Practice allowing as many people as possible to benefit from your powerful message.

As business women, we have an obligation to all other women to communicate our ideas so they can be found and used by people we may never personally meet. Imagine how the law of the universe will apply to you if you've helped people around the world with your message, people who can never possibly help you? That is when you know that your net is working at its optimum best!

Practice allowing as many people as possible to benefit from your powerful message.

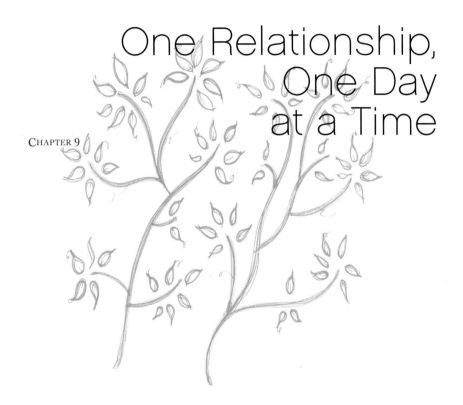

One Relationship, One Day at a Time

CHAPTER 9

One
Relationship
a Day
at a Time

In case at this point you are feeling down because you haven't capitalized on all the networking opportunities in your past, let me share with you a story, originally told by Jaroldeen Asplund Edwards. It is called "The Daffodil Principle," and it goes like this:

Several times my daughter, Carolyn, had telephoned me to say, 'Mother, you must come to see the daffodils before they are over.' I wanted to go, but it was a two-hour drive from Laguna to Lake Arrowhead, where my daughter lived. 'I'll come next Tuesday,' I promised reluctantly on our third call. The next Tuesday dawned cold and rainy. Still, I had promised her I'd be there, so I drove the distance. When I finally walked in to Carolyn's house and hugged and greeted my grandchildren, I said that we should forget the daffodils that day because the road was invisible in the clouds and fog. 'There was nothing in the world except you and these children that I would want to see bad enough to drive another inch in this weather.' My daughter smiled calmly and said that she drove in this kind of weather all the time. 'Even so,' I told her, 'you won't get me back on the road until it clears and then I am heading for home.' 'Okay, Mom', she said, 'but I was hoping you would take me over to the garage to pick up my car before you go. It's just a few blocks and I'll drive, I'm used to this.' A few minutes after we left in the car, it was clear we weren't on our way to the garage. 'We are going to the garage the long way,' Carolyn smiled '…by way of the daffodils.' 'Please turn around,' I said sternly. 'It's all right, Mother,' she said, 'I promise you will never forgive yourself if you miss this experience.'

After about 20 minutes we turned onto a short gravel road and I saw a small church. On the far side of the church I saw a hand-lettered sign that read Daffodil Garden. We got out of the car and we each took a child's hand and walked down the path. As we turned the corner of the path, I looked up and gasped. Before me lay the most glorious sight. It looked as though someone had taken a great vat of gold and poured it down over the mountain peak and slopes. The flowers were planted in majestic swirling patterns, great ribbons and swaths of deep orange, white, lemon yellow, salmon pink, saffron, and butter yellow. Each different colored variety was planted as a group so that it swirled and flowed like it was its own river with its own unique hue. There were five acres of flowers. 'But who has done this?' I asked Carolyn. 'It is just one woman,' she answered. 'She lives on the property. That is her home.' Carolyn pointed to a well-kept A-frame house that looked small and modest in the midst of all that glory. We walked up to the house. On the patio we saw a poster. 'Answers to the questions I know you are asking' was the headline. The first line was a simple one: '50,000 bulbs,' it read. The second answer was, 'One at a time, by one woman, two hands, two feet and a very little brain.' The third answer was, 'It began in 1958.'

That was a life-changing moment. I thought of this woman whom I had never met, but who more than 40 years before had begun, one bulb at a time, to bring her vision of beauty and joy to an obscure mountain top. Just planting one bulb at a time, year after year, had changed the world. She had created something of magnificence, beauty, and inspiration. The principle her daffodil garden taught is one of the greatest principles of celebration. That is, learning to move toward our goals and desires one step at a time, often just one baby step at a time, and learning to *love the doing. When we multiply tiny pieces of time with small increments of daily effort, we too will find we can accomplish magnificent things. We can change the world.*

'It makes me sad in a way,' I admitted to Carolyn. 'What might I have accomplished, if I had thought of a wonderful goal 35 or 40 years ago and had worked away at it, one bulb at a time, through all those years? Just think what I might have been able to achieve.' My daughter summed up the message of the day in her usual direct way. 'Start tomorrow,' she said. 'It is so pointless to think of the lost hours of yesterdays. The way to make learning this a lesson of celebration instead of a cause for regret is to only ask, "How I can put this to use today?"

The point is that it is never too late to start building a robust and vast network. Don't dwell on missed opportunities, but rather, think of the things you can do today. Plant the seeds of success today that will blossom into wonderful opportunities and tremendous abundance tomorrow.

Next Steps to Building Your Network

CHAPTER 10

Next Steps
Building
your
Network

Here is a quick recap of the main points of this book and some ideas about how to begin the process that will make you a successful relationship networker.

- Create a business card with nothing on the back so you can easily write down a tip or lead. Then your card becomes as valuable as gold.

- Learn the art of conversation, especially how to start a conversation any time with a complete stranger.

- Discover an attitude of abundance. Our philosophy at eWomenNetwork is that the giving comes first, and the getting comes second.

- Make sure you have a strong business presence, meaning, a way to keep attracting business even while you are out doing business.

- Don't worry about relationships you might have missed out on in the past. Instead, focus on making a difference today.

I'm often asked, "How do you really know whether you have a viable and solid network?" When it comes to networking, it's not at all about the number of names and addresses you have—that is only a database. Your network is defined very differently. Here's a clever way to measure whether you have a powerful relationship network. Ask yourself this question: "If you were arrested today for networking effectively, would there be enough evidence to convict you?" Imagine for a moment the number of people who would be passionate to speak as your witnesses, to stand in line in the cold, rain, or blistering heat, so they could convince a jury that they know from personal experience that you are guilty— guilty of helping others achieve their dreams. Now, if the number of witnesses in your defense is small, don't worry. Just think of the opportunity that is in front of you!

So now it's your turn. I've got ten exercises to help you get started to become the powerful relationship networker I know you can be. I would encourage you to write your own notes in the space below each exercise. Write your next opportunity to accomplish each challenge, and then come back and jot down the date and your thoughts after you've done each one.

1. Write your own 15 to 20 second introduction and practice it in front of the mirror at least ten times, or until you've got it memorized and can say it with confidence and a smile. Don't operate in a vacuum. Ask others for feedback and incorporate their suggestions and ideas for improvement.

....

....

....

....

....

....

....

....

....

....

2. Think of three places you are already going in the next week that you can turn into networking opportunities. It could be as simple as the grocery store or as fabulous as a big event. Smile, start a conversation and practice using the ex-words I've shared with you—example, explain, expand in order to establish a connection. After someone helps you, commit to practicing "sweet revenge"—make sure you "get even" by trying to identify opportunities to help them in return.

....

....

....

....

....

....

....

....

....

3. Remember back over the last year, and think of two people whom you keep meaning to bring together. Send each a note of introduction to the other. Better yet, splurge by offering to connect them both at a local coffee house. Stay for 20 to 30 minutes to make the introductions, start the conversation, and ensure that rapport and connection has been established. Then excuse yourself early and let the connection between the two you've introduced take on a life of its own as they begin to collaborate.

....

....

....

....

....

....

....

....

....

....

4. Go back over the last month and recall all the times you networked. Were there promises you made to someone that you just haven't had time to keep, or for some other reason neglected to keep? Don't procrastinate one more minute. Make that happen today.

....

....

....

....

....

....

....

....

....

....

....

5. Find a new networking opportunity in your area and sign up for their next event. Consider it as an investment in getting an education on how to develop mastery in building connections and expanding your network. Chances are the investment you make in this education is far less than the investment you've made in your own education—whether through the local university or the school of hard knocks. Practice your new style of networking, letting your new connections know who you are and what you need, and that you are what they need, too.

....

....

....

....

....

....

....

....

6. Take inventory of your networking constituents. Discover any gaps in your network. Develop a plan that focuses on the strategies you will follow in order to address these gaps within a certain period of time.

....

....

....

....

....

....

....

....

....

....

....

....

....

7. Send a thank-you in one form or another to two people who specifically helped you get business in the last few months. Buy a number of thank-you cards, put stamps on the blank envelopes, and stash them in a variety of places (such as the glove compartment in your car, your journal, a desk drawer, and your purse). Start the habit of sending at least two or three thank-you notes a week. It may seem like a monumental task at first, but you will soon learn to incorporate that action into your day.

....

....

....

....

....

....

....

....

....

....

8. Send out notes to two people you admire as role models, and tell them why you admire them. If possible, send a newspaper or magazine article you think they would particularly enjoy. Find out their philanthropic passion and offer to get involved as well.

....

....

....

....

....

....

....

....

....

....

....

....

9. Consider three things you plan to buy in the next month — small or large—and see whether you can find women-owned or women-run businesses in your area to buy from. Don't hesitate to let them know that part of your decision to do business with them is because you want to support women. Get good service somewhere? Make sure you tell ten other women about it!

....

....

....

....

....

....

....

....

....

....

....

....

10. Take a look at your business presence. How many avenues do you have in place to attract business? How easy is it for others to find you? What ways do you have of doing business while you're out attracting new business? List several you have and several you'd like to develop (your web site, a new brochure, products such as books and CDs). Set a goal and make a plan of action.

....

....

....

....

....

....

....

....

....

....

....

As I close, let me just say that networking should be fun. Learning how to converse, connect, collaborate, and create requires a set of skills. The good news is, if you don't have the set of skills to effectively network, you can learn them and yes, it's just like riding a bike! The more you practice, the better you will get. There will be instances, I'm sure, where things will not always work out as you envisioned. Like riding a bike, you're going to fall on occasion and maybe even fall and bruise yourself or bruise a relationship, but that's not a reason to quit.

Developing great relationships and a solid network takes persistence and consistency. Now you have either learned or enhanced your skills at inviting conversation, creating connections, and developing ways to collaborate that will evolve into the creation of new ideas, strategies, business, colleagues, and friends. The opportunities will be endless and the results will be profound. My wish for you is a world of wonderful new relationships and great connections. Have fun!

Endnotes and Resources

1 U.S. Census Bureau
2 U.S. Small Business Administration
3 WOW Quick Facts, 2005
4 U.S. Small Business Administration
5 Center for Women's Business Research
6 Kauffman Foundation
7 Kauffman Foundation
8 Catalyst, Census of Women Board Directors, 2003
9 WOW Quick Facts, 2005

Thanks to the above organizations and publications for the statistics in this book. For more information about women and women in business, see their web sites.

U.S. Census Bureau – www.census.gov
U.S. Small Business Administration – www.sba.gov
Tom Peters, Re-Imagine, 2003 – www.tompeters.com
WOW Quick Facts, Business Women's Network, 2005 –
        www.wowquickfacts.com
Center for Women's Business Research – www.nfwbo.org
Ewing Marian Kauffman Foundation – www.emkf.org
Catalyst – www.catalystwomen.org

What is eWomenNetwork?

- We are a women's media company providing a comprehensive suite of services to help women market and promote who they are and what they have to offer.
- We are the #1 resource for connecting and promoting women and their businesses worldwide.
- We help women access needed resources and create business relationships that move from interactions to transactions.

Events

- 90 Chapters throughout North America
- Over 1400 events produced annually
- Monthly Accelerated Networking™ events
- Breakthroughs Over Breakfast™
- Strategic Business Introductions™
- Annual International Conference & Business Expo

Broadcast Media

- #1 women's business radio show, broadcast on the largest ABC affiliate in the United States
- eWomenSpeakersNetwork

Print Media

- eWomenPublishingNetwork
- Largest women's magazine publishing alliance in North America

Foundation

- 501(c) (3) non-profit
- Helps women and girls in need
- Awards cash grants
- Provides education programs
- Gives International Femtor™ Awards

eWomenNetwork.com Web Site

- Most-visited business women's web site in North America
- 200,000 hits daily
- Largest photographic database of North American business women

Want to join us?

Find a chapter near you at

www.eWomenNetwork.com

Corporate Headquarters:
   Dallas, Texas   972-620-9995

Get to Know Sandra Yancey

Sandra Yancey is the Founder & CEO of eWomenNetwork, Inc., a women's media company, and the #1 resource for connecting and promoting women and their businesses worldwide. She is an international speaker and a leading authority in the areas of business, networking, communication and leadership.

Headquartered in Dallas, Texas, and founded in 2000, eWomenNetwork is the fastest growing membership-based women's business network in North America. eWomenNetwork has pioneered a whole new way for women to promote themselves and achieve their business objectives. The organization, with a database of over 500,000 female business owners and executives, has 15,000 members and conducts more than 1,400 events annually in cities across North America. The eWomenNetwork.com web site receives over 200,000 hits daily, making it the most visited business women's web site in the U.S. and Canada.

eWomenNetwork's mission is to help women market and promote who they are and what they have to offer. The objective is to create a vast network of women helping women achieve, succeed and prosper. Of over 7,000 women's organizations ranked by Business Women's Network International (BWNI), eWomenNetwork was selected the #1 most effective online women's network in North America.

Sandra hosts the #1 rated "eWomenNetwork Radio Show," which broadcasts weekly out of Dallas, Texas on the largest ABC radio affiliate in the U.S., 820 WBAP. The program provides the only national platform for showcasing the brilliance of business women.

Sandra Yancey holds a Master's degree in Organization Development from American University in Washington D.C., and completed a two-year post-graduate program in Organization and Systems Development from the Gestalt Institute in Cleveland, Ohio. She is the recipient of numerous national business awards including the 2005 Entrepreneurial Star award from Business Women's Network International and Microsoft, the 2005 Woman Advocate of the Year award from Women's Regional Publications of America and the 2006 Enterprising Women Advocacy Award for outstanding advocacy on behalf of women-owned enterprises from *Enterprising Women Magazine*. Sandra's story and her advice for business women is featured in *Chicken Soup for the Entrepreneur's Soul* (2006).

The eWomenNetwork Foundation has awarded hundreds of thousands of dollars in cash grants, in-kind donations and support to women's non-profit organizations and scholarships for emerging female leaders of tomorrow.

Index